Student Writing Handbook

Being a
Writer™

SECOND EDITION

First edition published 2007. Second edition 2014.

Being a Writer is a trademark of Center for the Collaborative Classroom.

Center for the Collaborative Classroom wishes to thank the following authors, agents, and publishers for their permission to reprint materials included in this program. Every effort has been made to trace the ownership of copyrighted material and to make full acknowledgment of its use. If errors or omissions have occurred, they will be corrected in subsequent printings, provided that notification is submitted in writing to the publisher.

"I'm Sorry" and "I'm Much Too Tired To Play Tonight" © 1990 by Jack Prelutsky from *Something Big Has Been Here* by Jack Prelutsky, used by permission of HarperCollins Publishers. "The Fly Is In" © 1981 by Evil Eye Music, Inc. From *A Light in the Attic* by Shel Silverstein, used by permission of HarperCollins Publishers. Excerpts from "The Missing Moon" and "A Snake Named Moon" from *The Moon and I* by Betsy Byars. Copyright © 1991, published by Simon & Schuster. Reproduced by permission of the author. "Little Things" copyright © 2002 by Sara Roberts and excerpt from "The Mirror" copyright © 2002 by Jijo Vilayanickal. Reprinted by permission of TeenInk.com. "Hot Rolls" and "Learning the Hard Way" from *Childtimes: A Three-Generation Memoir* copyright © 1979 by Eloise Greenfield and Lessie Jones Little. Used by permission of HarperCollins Publishers. Excerpts from *Miss Rumphius* by Barbara Cooney, copyright © 1982 by Barbara Cooney Porter. Used by permission of Viking Penguin, a division of Penguin Group (USA) LLC. Excerpts from *Roxaboxen*, text copyright © 1991 by Alice McLerran. Used by permission of HarperCollins Publishers. Excerpts from *Morning on the Lake* written by Jan Bourdeau Waboose and illustrated by Karen Reczuch. Used by permission of Kids Can Press Ltd., Toronto. Text copyright © 1997 Jan Bourdeau Waboose. Excerpt from *Owl Moon* by Jane Yolen, text copyright © 1987 by Jane Yolen. Used by permission of Philomel Books, a division of Penguin Group (USA) LLC. Excerpts from *The Day of Ahmed's Secret* copyright © 1990 by Florence Parry Heide and Judith Heide Gilliland, used by permission of HarperCollins Publishers. Excerpt from *Night of the Gargoyles* by Eve Bunting. Text copyright © 1991 by Eve Bunting. Reprinted by permission of Clarion Books, an imprint of Houghton Mifflin Harcourt Publishing Company. All rights reserved. "About the Author" from *Mexico* by Colleen Sexton. Copyright © 2011 by Colleen Sexton. Used by permission of Bellwether Media. All rights reserved. Excerpt from *Children's Quick and Easy Cookbook* by Angela Wilkes (Dorling Kindersley, 1997, 2006). Copyright © 1997, 2003 Dorling Kindersley Ltd. Text copyright © 1997 Angela Wilkes. Excerpt from *The Jumbo Vegetarian Cookbook* written by Judi Gillies and Jennifer Glossop and illustrated by Louise Phillips is used by permission of Kids Can Press Ltd., Toronto. Text © 2002 Judi Gillies and Jennifer Glossop. Illustrations © 2002 Louise Phillips. Excerpt from *1-2-3 Draw Cartoon People* by Steve Barr. Copyright © 2004, published by Peel Productions, www.123draw.com. Reprinted by permission of Peel Productions. Reproductions from *Drawing Cartoons* by permission of Usborne Publishing, 83-85 Saffron Hill, London EC1N 8RT, UK, www.usborne.com. Distributed in the USA by EDC Publishing, 10302 E. 55th Place, Tulsa, OK 74146, www.edcpub.com. Copyright © 2002 Usborne Publishing Ltd. Excerpt from *The Book of Cards for Kids*. Text copyright © 1992 by Gail MacColl. Art copyright © 1992 by Simms Taback. Reprinted by permission of Workman Publishing Company. "1,2,3 Dragon" and "Catching Stars" from www.ga.k12.pa.us. Copyright © 1996 by Germantown Academy. Used by permission of Germantown Academy. All rights reserved. "Feeling Ill" and "Over My Toes" from *The Best of Michael Rosen* by Michael Rosen. Copyright © 1995 Michael Rosen. Used by permission of Dewey Decimal Productions. All rights reserved. "Lullaby" from *Old Elm Speaks: Tree Poems* by Kristine O'Connell George. Copyright © 1998 by Kristine O'Connell George. Reprinted by permission of Clarion Books, an imprint of Houghton Mifflin Harcourt Publishing Company. All rights reserved. "lawnmower," "cow," and "mosquito" from *All the Small Poems and Fourteen More*. Copyright © 1994 by Valerie Worth. Reprinted by permission of Farrar, Straus and Giroux, LLC. All rights reserved. "Windy Nights" by Rodney Bennett appears in *Knock at a Star* copyright © 1999, edited by X. J. Kennedy and Dorothy M. Kennedy, published by Little, Brown and Company. "Up and Down" from *Autumnblings*. Text copyright © 2003 Douglas Florian. Used by permission of HarperCollins Publishers. "Egg" from *The Great Frog Race and Other Poems* by Kristine O'Connell George. Copyright © 1997 by Kristine O'Connell George. Reprinted by permission of Houghton Mifflin Harcourt Publishing Company. All rights reserved. "Crickets" from *I Never Told and Other Poems* by Myra Cohn Livingston. Copyright © 1992 by Myra Cohn Livingston. Used by permission of Marian Reiner.

All articles and texts reproduced in this manual and not referenced with a credit line above were created by Center for the Collaborative Classroom.

Cover illustration by Michael Wertz

Center for the Collaborative Classroom
1001 Marina Village Parkway, Suite 110
Alameda, CA 94501
(800) 666-7270; fax: (510) 464-3670
collaborativeclassroom.org

ISBN 978-1-61003-256-8

Printed in the United States of America

20 21 22 BNG 26 25 24 23 22 21

Center for the Collaborative Classroom is a nonprofit, mission-driven organization that supports collaboration and innovation among educators. In order to protect our intellectual property and prevent misrepresentation of our unique approach to literacy instruction and the classroom community, we respectfully ask that you do not copy, reuse, or modify the material herein for use on any third-party lesson-sharing websites.

Being a Writer™

SECOND EDITION

I'm Sorry!
by Jack Prelutsky

I'm sorry I squashed a banana in bed,
I'm sorry I bandaged a whole loaf of bread,
I'm sorry I pasted the prunes to your pants,
I'm sorry I brought home the ants.

I'm sorry for letting the dog eat the broom,
I'm sorry for freeing a frog in your room,
I'm sorry I wrote on the wall with sardines,
I'm sorry I sat on the beans.

I'm sorry for putting the peas in my hair,
I'm sorry for leaving the eggs on your chair,
I'm sorry for tying a can to the cat,
I'm sorry for being a brat!

Poem

I'm Much Too Tired to Play Tonight
by Jack Prelutsky

I'm much too tired to play tonight,
I'm much too tired to talk,
I'm much too tired to pet the dog
or take him for a walk,
I'm much too tired to bounce a ball,
I'm much too tired to sing,
I'm much too tired to try to think
about a single thing.

I'm much too tired to laugh tonight,
I'm much too tired to smile,
I'm much too tired to watch TV
or read a little while,
I'm much too tired to drink my milk
or even nod my head,
but I'm not nearly tired enough
to have to go to bed.

The Fly Is In
by Shel Silverstein

The fly is in
The milk is in
The bottle is in
The fridge is in
The kitchen is in
The house is in
The town.

The flea is on
The dog is on
The quilt is on
The bed is on
The carpet is on
The floor is on
The ground.

The worm is under
The ground is under
The grass is under
The blanket is under
The diaper is under
The baby is under
The tree.

The bee is bothering
The puppy is bothering
The dog is bothering
The cat is bothering
The baby is bothering
Mama is bothering
Me.

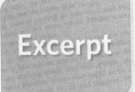

from "The Missing Moon"

in *The Moon and I* by Betsy Byars

I heard a noise.

I got up and glanced over the porch railing. There was the snake on the ground, cornered in an angle of the chimney. A neighbor's calico cat—Ginger—held it in place.

My heart actually leapt, like in poetry.

Thank you, Ginger.

Ginger and the snake were involved in a tense, eyeball-to-eyeball face-off.

The sounds I had heard were coming from the cat. These were low, throaty growls that couldn't have had much effect because snakes don't have ears.

The snake remained coiled, silent, alert, and ready. The tip of its tail began to quiver.

Perhaps, I thought, the snake was gearing up for one of those brave, absurd fights my husband had spoken of. I was torn between wanting to see the snake in action and not wanting to see it bite its own body.

Like a mother whose child is threatened, I slapped my hands against the side of the railing.

"Go home, Ginger!"

The cat looked up, startled. Then she dashed into the woods, taking the shortcut for home.

My snake remained for a moment, testing the climate with flicks of its dark, forked tongue. Then, apparently satisfied that the danger had passed, the snake began uncoiling.

(continues)

Excerpt from "The Missing Moon" *(continued)*

The black color was startling against the green ivy, and I could see that the snake was longer than I had thought—about six feet.

The snake began to move in a series of graceful S-curves, its head a few inches off the ground.

It circled the chimney. The movement was as slick as mercury.

Excerpt from *The Moon and I* by Betsy Byars. Copyright © 1991, published by Simon & Schuster. Reproduced by permission of the author.

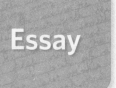

Essay

Little Things
by Sara Roberts
excerpted from *Teen Ink: What Matters*

Always and in everything let there be reverence.

— *Confucius*

My grandmother, whom I call Gramcracker, has taught me so many amazing things. My favorite was how, when she was a little girl, the smallest things meant so much to her. I envy that about her. In our generation, not many people think that way. Everything is "I have" or "I want." No one really appreciates the little things in life.

I often sit with Gramcracker and talk about everyday things. One time outside, I was talking with her, and a beautiful, brilliantly colored monarch butterfly flew past us. I really didn't think about it, but Gramcracker certainly did. She said, "That monarch reminds me of when I was little." So, of course, like every curious child, I asked her to tell me the story.

Gramcracker told me that when she was little and lived on a farm, there was a manure pile that for some reason attracted dozens of monarch butterflies. My grandma always wanted pretty, colorful curtains for her room, and so she had decided that she would pin dried butterflies on her curtains to make them beautiful. One day, she took a net and a jar and scooped a bunch into the jar, sealing it tight. My gramcracker hid them so her parents wouldn't find out. A few days later her parents called her downstairs saying, "Look what we found in our closet!" Gramcracker couldn't believe it. They had found her butterflies, but the once-beautiful butterflies were not beautiful anymore. Their wings were torn from trying to escape from the jar. They wouldn't make pretty curtains anymore. She felt horrible for killing them. She had

(continues)

"Little Things" copyright © 2002 by Sara Roberts. Reprinted by permission of TeenInk.com.

Little Things *(continued)*

wanted beautiful curtains so much that she had killed those butterflies just to get them. Yet she still felt sad because she wouldn't have her pretty curtains. From that day on, she learned to enjoy nature, not capture it.

I never forgot that story. Last Christmas I wanted to find something special for Gramcracker, so I made a wooden frame for a small window. Then I put cloth over the windows and tied them back like curtains. For the final touch, I put fake butterflies on the curtains, just as she had wanted all those years ago.

She couldn't believe that I had gone through so much trouble just to give her the curtains she always wanted. When I gave my gramcracker her present, she loved it so much that she started to cry.

I will never forget her story about the butterflies. I also will never forget how she showed me how to respect nature's beauty. I love my gramcracker so much for teaching me respect. I hope one day I can teach my grandchildren as many things as my gramcracker has taught me.

Opening Sentences from Three Personal Narratives

Every Sunday morning, Mama cooked a special breakfast. Beefsteak or pork chops, something like that. She and Papa had coffee or tea, and we had Postum. And rolls. Mama could make the best old rolls, they were some kind of good!

— from "Hot Rolls" (*Childtimes*)

Mama used to say, "You always have to learn things the hard way, don't you, Lessie?"

— from "Learning the Hard Way" (*Childtimes*)

I glanced up and saw it.
Snake, I said to myself. That looks like a snake.
I got up out of my porch rocking chair and went closer.
That *is* a snake.

— from "A Snake Named Moon" (*The Moon and I*)

Closing Sentences from Three Personal Narratives

I'd keep on until Papa said, "Little duckie"—that's what he called us—"Little duckie," he'd say, "if you eat any more, you won't be able to get out of your chair." And that would be the end of that.

— from "Hot Rolls" (*Childtimes*)

Now I understand that life always returns whatever you give. Your life is not a coincidence, but a mirror of your actions.

— from "The Mirror"

I will never forget her story about the butterflies. I also will never forget how she showed me how to respect nature's beauty. I love my gramcracker so much for teaching me respect. I hope one day I can teach my grandchildren as many things as my gramcracker has taught me.

— from "Little Things"

Excerpt

from *Miss Rumphius*
by Barbara Cooney

The next spring Miss Rumphius was not very well. Her back was bothering her again, and she had to stay in bed most of the time.

The flowers she had planted the summer before had come up and bloomed in spite of the stony ground. She could see them from her bedroom window, blue and purple and rose-colored.

"Lupines," said Miss Rumphius with satisfaction. "I have always loved lupines the best. I wish I could plant more seeds this summer so that I could have still more flowers next year."

But she was not able to.

After a hard winter spring came. Miss Rumphius was feeling much better. Now she could take walks again. One afternoon she started to go up and over the hill, where she had not been in a long time.

"I don't believe my eyes!" she cried when she got to the top. For there on the other side of the hill was a large patch of blue and purple and rose-colored lupines!

"It was the wind," she said as she knelt in delight. "It was the wind that brought the seeds from my garden here! And the birds must have helped!"

Then Miss Rumphius had a wonderful idea!

from *Roxaboxen*
by Alice McLerran

A town of Roxaboxen began to grow, traced in lines of stone: Main Street first, edged with the whitest ones, and then the houses. . . . At first the houses were very plain, but soon they all began to add more rooms. The old wooden boxes could be shelves or tables or anything you wanted. You could find pieces of pottery for dishes. Round pieces were best.

———————————————————————

After a while they added other streets. Frances moved to one of them and built herself a new house outlined in desert glass, bits of amber, amethyst, and sea-green: a house of jewels.

———————————————————————

Sometimes in the winter, when everybody was at school and the weather was bad, no one went to Roxaboxen at all, not for weeks and weeks. . . . And spring came, and the ocotillo blossomed, and everybody sucked the honey from its flowers, and everybody built new rooms, and everybody decided to have jeweled windows.

from *Morning on the Lake* (1)
by Jan Bourdeau Waboose

Grandfather stretches out his steady, strong arm. I hold onto it and climb into the canoe. It feels wobbly, so I sit very still. We begin to drift away from shore. Because I am in the front looking out, I cannot see my grandfather's face. But I know that he is smiling. I hear the dip of his paddle on the water and imagine many tiny bubbles trailing behind us on the glassy surface. I watch my reflection on the water as we glide.

It is still in the early morning. There is no wind and it feels cool and damp. Everything is silent, except for the sound of the paddle.

The morning is no longer serene and still. Birds chirp their morning songs across the lake. I sense the animals stirring on the shore. The mist is gone. The sun, full and warm, shines bright above the trees. The wind ripples the water. The leaves sway gently in the scented breeze.

Closing Sentences from Three Stories

When you go owling
you don't need words
or warm
or anything but hope.
That's what Pa says.
The kind of hope
that flies
on silent wings
under a shining
Owl Moon.

— from *Owl Moon*

"Look," I say. "Look, I can write my name."
I write my name over and over as they watch, and I think of my name now lasting longer than the sound of it, maybe even lasting, like the old buildings in the city, a thousand years.

— from *The Day of Ahmed's Secret*

More than fifty years later, Frances went back and Roxaboxen was still there. She could see the white stones bordering Main Street, and there where she had built her house the desert glass still glowed—amethyst, amber, and sea-green.

— from *Roxaboxen*

from *Morning on the Lake* (2)
by Jan Bourdeau Waboose

"Morning is calling. It is time."

I hear my grandfather's slow, quiet voice in the distance. There is no need for him to say it again. I jump out of bed, rub the sleep from my eyes and pull on my T-shirt and pants. As I run to the lake where he stands, waiting, I see his large silhouette against the pink morning sky. He is staring out at the cool, calm water. Morning mist looks like a gray blanket covering the lake. The sun is a big orange ball hiding behind the trees. I imagine it being pulled up by spiders' strings.

Point of View in Two Stories

Today I have a secret, and all day long my secret will be like a friend to me.

Tonight I will tell it to my family, but now I have work to do in my city.

My donkey pulls the cart I ride on. I have many stops to make today. The streets are crowded. Everyone is going somewhere. Like me, everyone has something important to do.

— from *The Day of Ahmed's Secret*

The gargoyles squat
high on corners
staring into space,
their empty eyes unblinking
till night comes.

Then there is movement
in the shadowy corners
as the gargoyles creep
on stubs of feet
along the high ledges
and peer,
nearsighted,
into rooms where mummies lie
in boxes, long and thin
as coffins, ribboned round
with painted boats and figures
dark as night.

— from *Night of the Gargoyles*

Speech Punctuation in Two Stories

In the evening Alice sat on her grandfather's knee and listened to his stories of faraway places. When he had finished, Alice would say, "When I grow up, I too will go to faraway places, and when I grow old, I too will live beside the sea."

"That is all very well, little Alice," said her grandfather, "but there is a third thing you must do."

"What is that?" asked Alice.

"You must do something to make the world more beautiful," said her grandfather.

"All right," said Alice. But she did not know what that could be.

— from *Miss Rumphius*

Instead of telling them about my day, I say, "Look, I have something to show you."

It is time to tell my secret. I take a deep breath.

"Look," I say. "Look, I can write my name."

— from *The Day of Ahmed's Secret*

Punctuation for Effect in Three Stories

After a hard winter spring came. Miss Rumphius was feeling much better. Now she could take walks again. One afternoon she started to go up and over the hill, where she had not been in a long time.

"I don't believe my eyes!" she cried when she got to the top. For there on the other side of the hill was a large patch of blue and purple and rose-colored lupines!

— from *Miss Rumphius*

Very still, we wait, perched on top of our rocky nest. I can hear my own breathing. It is loud. I cannot hear Grandfather's. I wonder if he is holding his breath. I want to look at him, take one quick peek. But then . . . I see a powerful bird in slow motion. Alone and gliding.

— from *Morning on the Lake*

There were two ice cream parlors. Was Paul's ice cream the best, or Eleanor's? Everybody kept trying them both. (In Roxaboxen you can eat all the ice cream you want.)

— from *Roxaboxen*

Excerpts

Closing Sentences from Three Informational Reports

A *Francophile* is someone who loves France and everything about it, from the Eiffel Tower to those buttery, melt-in-your-mouth croissants. Has reading this report turned you into a Francophile? I hope so! As they say in France, *à bientôt*. (That is pronounced "ah bee-en-toh" and it means "See you soon.")

— by Monica

As you have learned, Haiti has not had it easy. The 2010 earthquake was devastating, and most Haitians are very poor. But as you have also learned, Haiti is a country filled with rhythmic music and joyful dance, a country where parents treasure their children above all else.

— by Anthony

With all its amazing artifacts and monuments—the Rosetta Stone, the Pyramids, and the Great Sphinx, to name just a few—it's easy to understand why tourism is one of the top ways Egypt makes money. From the days of the pharaohs to our own times, Egypt has remained one of the world's most interesting cultures. I hope you have enjoyed this exploration of a great civilization.

— by Lacey

Excerpt

from *Mexico*
by Colleen Sexton

About the Author

Colleen Sexton has a bachelor's degree in English from the College of Saint Benedict in St. Joseph, Minnesota. As a children's book editor, she focused on geography. She worked on books about countries and cultures around the world.

Colleen has written more than 100 nonfiction books for kids, ranging from biographies of J. K. Rowling and Jackie Robinson to series about space and deadly animals. But geography is still her favorite topic to write about.

Carrot Salad

from *Children's Quick and Easy Cookbook* by Angela Wilkes

⏱ 15 MINUTES   🍴 SERVES 4

CARROT SALAD

You will need

Cutting board • Kitchen brush or
vegetable peeler • Grater • Cookie sheet
Lemon squeezer • Small jar with lid
Salad bowl with servers

For the salad

6 large carrots

1 tablespoon
sunflower seeds

½ cup (85 g) raisins

For the dressing

½ orange

½ lemon

1 teaspoon
honey

3 tablespoons
hazelnut or olive oil

¼ teaspoon prepared French mustard

Salt and pepper

Decorate the salad by
sprinkling a few extra
raisins and sunflower
seeds over the top.

What to do

1 Scrub or peel the carrots and grate them coarsely. Toast the sunflower seeds lightly under the broiler for a few minutes.

2 Squeeze the juice out of the orange and lemon. Put the dressing ingredients into a jar, screw on the lid, and shake well.

3 Put the carrot, sunflower seeds, and raisins into a salad bowl. Pour the dressing over the top and toss the salad.

51

Carrot and Raisin Salad

from *The Jumbo Vegetarian Cookbook* by Judi Gillies and Jennifer Glossop

Carrot and Raisin Salad

When there's no lettuce in the fridge for salad, don't despair. Make this crunchy salad with just a few ingredients you probably have on hand.

You Will Need

4	carrots, peeled and grated	4
125 mL	raisins	1/2 cup
125 mL	peeled, cored and chopped apple	1/2 cup
50 mL	chopped nuts (optional)	1/4 cup
15 mL	lemon juice	1 tbsp.
Dressing		
50 mL	mayonnaise	1/4 cup
50 mL	lemon juice or vinegar	1/4 cup
	salt and pepper to taste	

Utensils

chef's knife	small bowl
measuring cup and spoons	whisk or fork
potato peeler	wooden spoon
grater (use larger holes)	juicer
mixing bowl	

1. In a mixing bowl, combine carrots, raisins, apple, nuts and lemon juice. Toss together.

2. Put the dressing ingredients in a small bowl. Beat with a whisk or fork until well mixed.

3. Pour over the carrot mixture. Toss well.

**Level:
Intermediate**

**Makes:
4 servings**

**Preparation:
15 minutes**

**with tofu
mayonnaise**

Salads • 115

Expressions and Emotions

from *1-2-3 Draw Cartoon People* by Steve Barr

Expressions and Emotions

In these drawings, can you see how eyes and mouths show feelings?
Experiment with different shapes and lines when you draw mouths
and eyes. Have fun! Discover for yourself what looks cool! For now,
though, let's try a few basic facial expressions...

Happy

Angry

Sad

Surprised

Silly

Really Happy!

Expressions

from *Drawing Cartoons* by Anna Milbourne

Expressions

An essential part of drawing cartoons is being able to draw expressions. You can draw lots of different expressions very simply. Then, you can use these to create complete cartoon characters.

> ☞ Take an online lesson in how to draw some simple faces. Or, play a game online, adding parts to a potato to create funny faces. For a link to these Web sites, go to **www.usborne-quicklinks.com**

A basic face

1. Draw a rough oval shape. It needn't be too neat. If it's lopsided it will add character.

2. Draw two small ovals for eyes, and put dots in them. Add a curve for a mouth.

Changing expressions

Using just the eyes and mouth on a face, you can draw all sorts of expressions. Copy the faces on the fruit below and try combining different eyes and mouths to vary their expressions.

Grinning
Surprised
Bashful
Sleepy
Sad
Laughing
Mischievous
Angry

6

Making a character

from *Drawing Cartoons* by Anna Milbourne

Making a character

A basic circle face, with just a mouth and eyes, already has lots of personality. Without adding much more, you can make simple cartoon characters. For example, just add legs to make a spider, or add wings and legs to make a flying insect.

In a cartoon garden, even the flowers can have faces.

Authors

from *The Book of Cards for Kids* by Gail MacColl

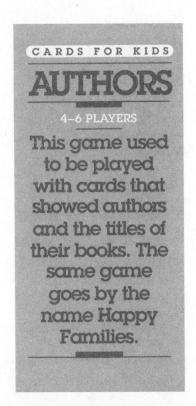

CARDS FOR KIDS

AUTHORS

4–6 PLAYERS

This game used to be played with cards that showed authors and the titles of their books. The same game goes by the name Happy Families.

OBJECT OF THE GAME

To collect as many books as possible. A book is all four cards of the same number or letter, one from each suit.

SET UP

ALL PLAYERS: Pick a card from the deck. The player with the highest card deals.

START

DEALER: Shuffle the cards. Deal out all the cards, one at a time and face down. It's all right if some players have more cards than others.

ALL PLAYERS: Look at your cards. Arrange them so that cards with the same number are side by side in your hand.

PLAY

PLAYER ON DEALER'S LEFT: You go first. Decide what cards you need to make a book. Ask one of the other players for one of those cards. You must ask for the exact card—for instance, the 9♠.

ALL PLAYERS: If you are asked for a card and you have it, you must hand it over. But if you only have a similiar card—for instance, the 9♣—say, "No."

Warning: If you say you don't have a card when you do, you'll pay a penalty when the other players find out—you'll have to give one of your cards to each of the other players.

● Play goes around to the left, with each player asking for cards and collecting books.

● When you have a book of four matching cards, show it to the other players, then put it face down in front of you.

● If you run out of cards by making a book, you must sit out the rest of the game. You will still count up the number of books you collected for scoring at the end of the game.

● When all the books have been collected and everyone is out of cards the game is over. The player with the most books is the winner.

PLAYER ON DEALER'S LEFT: When everyone has finished counting their books, gather up the cards. You will deal the next game.

STRATEGY

Pay attention! Listen to what other players are asking for, even if they aren't asking you. If you hear a player ask for the 7♦, for instance, you'll know she's trying to make a book of Sevens. If you are also collecting Sevens, you'll ask that player for her Sevens when your turn comes around.

1, 2, 3 Dragon
by students at Germantown Academy, PA

State the name of your game and why you chose it.

The name of the game is 1, 2, 3 Dragon. We chose it because it can include everyone, because it's tiring, because of its simplicity, and because it looked fun and challenging.

List the countries where it is played and its origin.

Variations of the game are played all over the world, but with different rules, scoring, and names.

1, 2, 3 Dragon originated in China and is played by small children, usually to celebrate the New Year. During the Chinese New Year they have dancing dragons, games and food. Dragons are important because they mean good luck.

Describe how your game is played. State the object of the game. Clearly describe the rules.

- 10 or more people form a line with each player holding the shoulders of the person in front of them.
- The person in the front is the "Head."
- The person at the back of the line is the "Tail."

To Begin:

- The tail shouts "1, 2, 3 dragon."
- The head leads the line and tries to catch the tail.
- The line must stay together the whole time.

(continues)

1, 2, 3 Dragon *(continued)*

End of a Round:

- If the dragon breaks, the dragon dies. The head moves to the end of the line and becomes the tail.
- If the head catches the tail, play stops and the head goes to the end of the line.
- The second person in line now becomes the head.

Object:

The object is to tag the tail as many times as you can while you are the head. A point is scored for each successful tag. Some people prefer to play without points.

List the equipment needed.

- 10 or more players.
- Playing area.
- Ages: 8 or older.

Catching Stars
by students at Germantown Academy, PA

State the name of your game and why you chose it.

We chose this game because we like the game "Mr. Fox" and this is very similar.

List the countries where it is played and its origin.

This game was developed by the pygmy tribes in Africa.

Describe how your game is played. State the object of the game. Clearly describe the rules.

- It takes seven or more players to play this game.

- Divide the players into two groups: Stars and Catchers

- Set up two boundaries about twenty feet apart.

- Catchers: stand in the middle of the two boundaries.

- Stars: stand on one side of the boundaries.

- Catchers: say "star light, star bright, how many stars are out tonight."

- Stars: say "more than you can catch!"

- The stars run across to the other end and try not to get tagged. The winner is the last person to get caught.

List the equipment needed.

- None. This is a simple running game.

Bugs Are Creepy

I think that bugs are creepy, gross, and annoying. I don't like them. In fact, I hate them.

When I say "bugs," I mean all insects and spiders. I think they are all creepy. For example, they are often furry with long skinny legs. Many have wiggly antennae, and some have wings and can fly. They look weird, like miniature aliens. Who knows, they might be aliens! I have no idea why they exist.

Another terrible thing about bugs is that bugs bite! Mosquitoes, spiders, ants, earwigs, and many other kinds of bugs bite. Some bugs like ticks or mosquitoes bite you to suck your blood. Yuck! Others bite you just to hurt you, whether you are going to kill them or not. One time, a tiny black ant bit me, and it really hurt. Some bug bites can even kill you, like a scorpion's bite and the bites of certain spiders like black widows. Also, you might die or get sick if you get stung by a bee and are allergic to bee stings.

Since bugs are everywhere, you can't get away from them. They are in the city, and they are in nature. For instance, you can find them on the sidewalk and in the dirt. They are in the garden under every rock and on the prettiest flowers. They are in your house. They are in your kitchen and on your food! Do you really feel like eating food after a fly has landed on it and taken a bite? Gross! Bugs even come out at night to fly around lights. I just can't get away from them!

As you can see, I think that bugs are strange, disgusting, and really annoying. I don't want to see them, touch them, or be bitten by them. I'm sure I'm not the only person who feels this way about bugs. . . . I bet you do, too!

Insects Are Amazing

I don't like when people call insects "bugs." That means that they bug them. Insects don't bug me. I actually think they are amazing. They are cool to watch, fun to play with, and interesting to learn about.

Insects are very important because they help plants and animals. For example, ladybugs eat aphids. Aphids eat the flowers in your garden. If you want a healthy garden, leave those ladybugs alone. Also, when an animal or a plant dies, insects eat it to help break it down. If you don't want a lot of smelly dead animals around, let those insects do their work. Also, many animals eat insects. I bet you think birds are beautiful. If there were no bugs, many birds would die because they need insects to eat.

Insects are also cool to watch and learn about. They do all sorts of cool things. For instance, ants can carry ten times their weight! In addition, ants and many other kinds of insects like bees can communicate without talking. They can tell each other where food is or where danger is by the way they move or by leaving scents. Have you ever watched all the moths that fly to a light at night? Why do they do that? How come they don't run into each other? These are the kinds of questions that entomologists (people who study insects) ask and get to figure out. That to me sounds like a pretty cool job.

Lastly, I don't see why insects are such a big deal since they don't usually bother people. Most insects live under rocks or in places that people don't always go. Most just want to be left alone. It seems to me that we should just leave them alone and let them

(continues)

Insects Are Amazing *(continued)*

do their work. When we do see them, we should just study them and learn more about them.

I hope you will think twice before you kill the next insect you see. That insect might be food for an animal, or it might be helping in some way you don't know about. Maybe, if you think twice, you will even agree with me that insects are amazing.

Helping Other Countries

Recently my class debated whether or not we should collect money to send to poor countries. I definitely think we should send money to other countries that need it. If we did, people in those countries could have things like clean water and they would see America as kind and caring. What seems like a little money to us is sometimes a lot of money to people in a poor country.

Here in America, we have so many things that the people in poor countries only dream about. We have toys for kids, schools, cars, clean water, nice clothes, and food. In many poor countries, kids and adults are dying because they are drinking polluted water or because they can't get the medicine they need. Sometimes there aren't any schools for the kids. Here in America, so many kids have fancy sneakers or video games that they don't need. What is more important: for you to be able to have the newest, hottest sneakers or for a family to be able to eat?

Also, if America would give some money to poorer countries, I think other countries would see that we are friendly and that we care. Maybe the world would be more peaceful if big countries like America shared some of their money with countries that need more.

Finally, a little amount of money to us is a lot to a person in a poor country. For example, if you bought a $40 pair of sneakers instead of a $60 pair, you could send $20 to a family so they could buy a goat. That goat would provide them with milk to drink with their meals. They would get vitamins that they need to help them be healthy. Also, the goat could have babies, and the family could eat some or sell them to buy other things.

(continues)

Helping Other Countries *(continued)*

If every person in America gave a little money, it would add up to a lot. It would make a big difference to people in other countries who don't have as much as we do. That's why I think that we should give money to help people in parts of the world that need help.

It Is Our Money and We Need It

Has there ever been a collection drive at your school urging you to give money to another country far away from the United States? Sometimes the money that is collected goes to build schools in other countries. The money also buys pencils and pays the salary of a teacher in a foreign country. I think that people in our country should not give money to help other countries for a few reasons.

We should not give our money away because our own schools need it. Many schools in this country don't have enough supplies. For example, our class usually doesn't have a supply of pencils to use. We have to bring pencils from home most of the time. I don't see why we should be expected to buy pencils for children in other countries when American children don't even have a steady supply of pencils. We should worry about ourselves before we worry about other countries.

Another reason we should keep our money is that the economy is bad in many parts of the United States. Thousands of people are losing their jobs and houses. The last thing we, as a country, need to be doing with our money is giving it away to pay a teacher's salary in a foreign country. I don't see how giving away our money for something that will not benefit our country is going to help our economy.

We have enough problems here, and we need to think about helping our own people first. For those reasons, I don't think the United States should give money to help other countries.

Bike Helmets

What do you think when you see a kid riding a bike without a helmet? Well, I think riding without a helmet is dangerous and people should wear a helmet every time they ride a bike.

First of all, it is the law. In most towns and cities, kids and teens have to wear a bike helmet every time they ride a bike. If they do not, they will be stopped by the police and their parents will be called. So if you don't want to be stopped by the police, wear your helmet.

When you are riding your bike on the street, you could get hit by a car. Cars go very fast, and when drivers pull out of parking spots and driveways, they might not see you riding your bike. If a car hits you, your head could hit the ground. If you are wearing a helmet, your head will be protected and the helmet will save your life.

Because bike helmets can prevent serious head injuries, parents and older kids should set a good example by wearing bicycle helmets when they ride. I know teens might not like the idea, but if everyone or almost everyone wears a helmet, kids won't think it is strange.

A bicycle helmet protects your head and could save your life if you fall off your bike. Also, it's the law for kids to wear helmets, and you don't want to break the law! So please wear your helmet every time you ride.

Volunteer work is very important in any community everyone should try doing some volunteer work, I think. There are many different kinds of volunteer work here are some examples. People can clean up local parks. They can help out at the public library they can tutor students in after-school programs. They can volunteer at a hospital.

_____

Volunteer work is a great way to meet new people it connects you to your community. When you volunteer, you meet other people from your city or neighborhood. You have fun together you get to know each other. Volunteer work is also great because it makes you feel proud and happy. You get a feeling of accomplishment because you are doing good things you may even learn some new skills.

Persuasive Essay Without Indentation

How much TV do you watch? Almost everybody watches some TV. Most people have a favorite show they enjoy viewing. That is fine, but I think that watching a lot of TV is not healthy or a good idea. People who watch too much TV sit around and don't get enough exercise. Our bodies need regular exercise to stay healthy. That's because exercise builds muscles. It helps people stay flexible. It also burns calories. Another big problem with TV is that it can be bad for people's brains. Watching too much TV makes people unable to concentrate or pay attention. TV is especially bad for young children's brains. It can change the way the brain works. In addition, watching TV takes time away from other important parts of life. If people watch a lot of TV, they are probably not talking to their friends or family. They are probably not going outside and enjoying nature. It's true that TV can be fun to watch. It is a nice way to relax sometimes. But I think you will agree with me that watching a lot of TV is bad for your body, bad for your brain, and bad for your life!

Feeling Ill

by Michael Rosen

Lying in the middle of the bed
waiting for the clock to change
flicking my toes on the sheets
watching an airplane cross the window
staring at the glare of the light
smelling the orange on the table
counting the flowers on the curtain
holding my head with my hand
hearing the steps on the stairs
lying in the middle of the bed
waiting for the clock to change.

Poem

Lullaby
by Kristine O'Connell George

Tree sighs softly
as the birds patter about
her heavy old branches,
settling down,
tucking their heads
beneath their wings.

She waits until dusk
has shadowed her leaves,
and when she's sure
she's heard that last
soft cheep,

she rocks her birds to sleep.

lawnmower
by Valerie Worth

The lawnmower
Grinds its teeth
Over the grass,
Spitting out a thick
Green spray;

Its head is too full
Of iron and oil
To know
What it throws
Away:

The lawn's whole
Crop of chopped
Soft,
Delicious
Green hay.

Windy Nights
by Rodney Bennett

Rumbling in the chimneys,
    Rattling at the doors,
Round the roofs and round the roads
    The rude wind roars;
Raging through the darkness,
    Raving through the trees,
Racing off again across
    The great grey seas.

Up and Down
by Douglas Florian

U^p in a tree
A screeching jay
Is teaching others:
Stay Away!
D
   o
     w
        n on the ground
A quiet squirrel
Buries acorns
For later referral.

Egg
by Kristine O'Connell George

There are
No tags, no tabs
Or wrapping paper,
Nor flaps, nor string,
Sticky tape or ribbon.
Never hidden up high
On a cupboard shelf.
Egg is a package
That can open
Itself.

Crickets
by Myra Cohn Livingston

they	tell
the	time
of	night
they	tick
the	time
of	night
they	tick
they	tell
of	night
they	tick
and	tell
the	time
they	tick
they	tell
the	time
they	click

Over My Toes
by Michael Rosen

Over my toes
goes
the soft sea wash
see the sea wash
the soft sand slip
see the sea slip
the soft sand slide
see the sea slide
the soft sand slap
the soft sand wash
over my toes.

cow
by Valerie Worth

The cow
Coming
Across the grass
Moves
Like a mountain
Toward us;
Her hipbones
Jut
Like sharp
Peaks
Of stone,
Her hoofs
Thump
Like dropped
Rocks:
Almost
Too late
She stops.

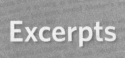

Poet Quotes: What Is Poetry?

"Poetry is things that are true expressed in words that are beautiful."

— Dante

"It takes probably hundreds of things coming together at the right moment to make a poem."

— Elizabeth Bishop

"Poetry is painting that is felt rather than seen."

— Leonardo da Vinci

"Poetry is the rhythmical creation of beauty in words."

— Edgar Allan Poe

"I know it's a poem if it blows the top of my head off."

— Robert Hass

Word Bank

about

absolutely

accidentally

ache

action

actually

addition

address

adjective

advice

afraid

Africa

again

against

agree

ahead

aid

all right

allow

almost

alone

along

already

although

always

among

amount

angle

answered

anything

apology

appear

apple

approximately

April

arctic

argue

arguing

argument

army

around

arrived

arrow

art

athlete

attack

aunt

author

awful

A

B

babble

backward

bacon

badge

bait

bank

bark

barn

basket

bass

bath

beach

bean

bear

beat

beautiful

because

been

before

beginning

believe

bell

belong

beside

bicycle

biggest

bit

blew

blind

block

blood

bloom

blow

blue

blunt

board

bold

bomb

bone

bones

boom

boost

bored

born

bottom

bought

bowl

bracelet

branches

break

breathe

bright

British

broken

brother

brown

build

built

buried

burn

burning

burst

bury

business

busy

buy

B

C

cab	celebrate	clue	cook
cabinet	cell	clump	cookie
cactus	cemetery	clumsy	cool
cage	center	cluster	copy
calf	cents	clutch	corn
calm	century	coast	corner
camel	chance	coffee	cost
camera	chart	coin	cotton
candle	chief	color	couldn't
cane	child	column	count
can't	children	comb	courageous
capital	chocolate	come	cows
captain	choose	comic	create
card	church	coming	crime
care	clean	company	crops
carrying	climbed	compare	cross
case	close	compound	crowd
catch	closet	conditions	cucumber
cattle	clothes	conquer	cupboard
caught	cloud	consider	curl
cause	cloudy	continued	current
ceiling	clown	control	cute

C

D

dairy

damp

dance

dangerous

dash

date

dead

deaf

deal

dear

death

decided

decimal

decision

deck

decorate

deer

defense

definitely

delay

dent

dentist

describe

desert

design

details

determine

developed

devour

dice

dictionary

died

difference

difficult

digest

dining

direct

direction

disappear

disappoint

discover

discovered

disease

distance

divided

division

doctor

does

doesn't

dollars

downpour

drawing

dress

drew

drive

dropped

drowned

dwarf

D

E

early	embarrass	equipment	except
ears	energy	especially	excitement
easy	engine	Europe	exciting
edge	England	evening	exercise
effect	enjoy	every	exhausted
eight	enough	everybody	expect
either	entered	everyone	experience
electric	entire	everything	experiment
elements	environment	exactly	express
else	equal	excellent	extremely

E

factories	fetch	flat	fraction
factors	fiddle	flavor	fracture
fail	fierce	flies	France
fair	fifteen	floor	freckle
faith	fig	flow	French
famous	fight	flowers	frenzy
farmer	finally	flute	fresh
farmers	fingers	folks	Friday
fascinate	finished	foot	friend
fault	first	football	fright
favorite	fit	forest	frigid
fear	flabby	forty	fruit
February	flag	forward	fuel
feeling	flannel	fossil	fun
fell	flash	fourth	fuss

F

G

gag	gel	goes	groan
gallon	general	gold	groove
gallop	gentle	gone	grumpy
gamble	germ	government	grunt
garbage	getting	grass	guard
garden	giant	greed	guess
gas	gift	Greek	guessed
gear	gigantic	grew	guilty
geese	glass	grind	gush

G

H

hail	haven't	hello	hospital
half	hay	herb	hour
handkerchief	health	here	house
hang	hear	heroes	huge
happened	heard	history	human
happy	heart	hit	hunting
hat	height	hope	
hatch	held	hoping	

I

igloo   industry   instruments   its
imaginary   information   interest   itself
impossible   innocent   interesting
increase   insects   iron
indicate   instead   isn't

J, K

jabber	jeans	kangaroo	knee
jacket	jeep	kept	knew
jail	jiffy	ketchup	knife
Japanese	jiggle	kettle	know
jaw	joined	key	knowledge
jazz	jumped	killed	

J, K

L

lady	lead	lettuce	located
lake	least	level	lose
lamp	led	library	losing
latch	legs	lick	lost
latter	length	lie	lot
laughed	leopard	lift	loud
law	lessons	lifted	loving
lawn	let's	lightning	lure
lay	letter	little	

L

M

magician	mask	melon	molecules
magnet	match	members	moment
magnificent	matter	metal	months
mail	maybe	method	moon
main	meadow	middle	morning
major	meal	million	mother
making	meat	mind	mouth
mammal	medicine	mine	movement
many	meet	minute	muscle
march	melody	modern	mysterious

M

N

name	neat	neigh	northern
nation	necessary	nice	nose
natural	necklace	none	
nature	needle	nor	

N

observe	office	opposite
o'clock	often	outside
off	once	oxygen

P

paid	peace	plural	prevent
pail	pear	poem	prince
pain	people	poison	princess
paint	per	pole	principal
pajamas	perhaps	pool	printed
palm	period	poor	prize
parade	phone	position	probably
paragraph	phrase	possible	process
park	picked	post	promise
parrot	piece	pounds	property
particular	piggyback	powder	provide
party	plains	prepared	purr
past	planets	present	pushed
paste	played	president	
patch	please	press	
pay	plum	pretend	

Q, R

quarter	raccoon	receive	return
quiet	race	received	rhythm
quit	radio	recommend	ribbon
quite	raft	record	rich
	rainbow	region	right
	raincoat	reindeer	ring
	raise	remain	rise
	raised	remember	rolled
	raisin	repeated	root
	ranch	report	rope
	rather	represent	rose
	rattle	responsibility	rough
	read	responsible	route
	ready	restaurant	row
	reason	result	running

Q, R

S

safe	shoes	snuggle	stone
safety	shop	soak	stopped
said	shoulder	soap	store
sail	shouted	soda	strange
sand	shriek	soil	stream
sandwich	shrink	soldier	stretch
Saturday	shy	soldiers	stretched
save	sigh	solution	string
says	sight	solve	students
scale	sign	some	studying
schedule	silent	somehow	subject
school	simple	someone	substances
schoolhouse	since	something	success
science	single	sometime	suddenly
scoop	sir	soon	suffix
score	sister	sorrow	sugar
seat	skin	soup	suggested
section	skinny	southern	sum
seeds	skis	speak	summer
sell	sleek	special	Sunday
send	sleep	speed	supply
sense	slick	spooky	suppose
sent	sling	spoon	sure
separate	slipper	spot	surely
serious	slope	sprain	surprise
serve	slow	spread	surrounded
settled	smash	spring	swat
seven	smear	sprinkle	sway
several	smell	square	swept
shall	smiled	squint	swim
sharp	smoky	statement	symbols
shining	snag	steel	
shock	snort	stick	

S

tail	thrill	tonight	truck
teacher	throat	too	truly
team	through	tools	tube
tear	thud	torn	Tuesday
temperature	thumb	total	tunnel
terms	thunder	touch	turtle
terrible	tide	tough	twig
their	tied	toward	twin
themselves	tiger	toys	twine
there	tight	track	twinkle
they	tiny	trade	twirl
thick	tired	trail	twist
thief	toad	train	twitch
thin	toast	treat	twitter
third	toe	triangle	two
thorn	together	tries	type
though	tomorrow	trip	
thought	tone	trouble	

T

_____

_____

_____

_____

_____

_____

_____

_____

_____

_____

_____

_____

_____

_____

_____

_____

_____

_____

_____

_____

_____

_____

_____

_____

U, V

uncle

underline

until

used

using

usually

vacation

valley

value

various

vegetable

vein

victim

view

village

visit

U, V

W

waist	we're	wild	wonder
wall	western	win	won't
wash	when	window	workers
Washington	where	wings	would
wasn't	whether	winter	wouldn't
weather	which	wipe	wreck
weigh	white	wire	write
weight	whole	wish	writing
weird	whose	within	written
we'll	wide	woman	wrong
were	wife	women	wrote

X, Y, Z

yard   zany

yellow   zap

yonder   zebra

you

your

you're

yummy

X, Y, Z

Proofreading Notes

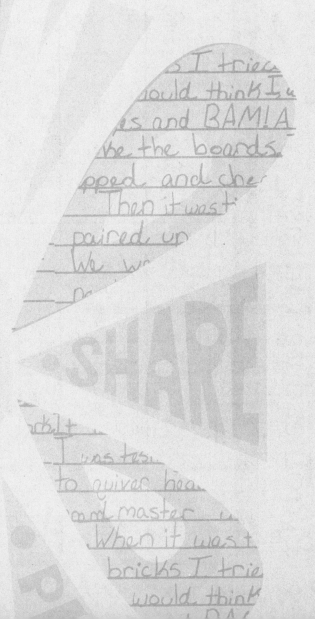

Proofreading Notes

✓	Rule	Example	Notes
☐			
☐			
☐			
☐			
☐			
☐			
☐			

Proofreading Notes

✓	Rule	Example	Notes
☐			
☐			
☐			
☐			
☐			
☐			
☐			

Proofreading Notes

✓	Rule	Example	Notes
☐			
☐			
☐			
☐			
☐			
☐			
☐			

Proofreading Notes

✓	Rule	Example	Notes
☐			
☐			
☐			
☐			
☐			
☐			
☐			

Proofreading Notes

✓	Rule	Example	Notes
☐			
☐			
☐			
☐			
☐			
☐			
☐			

Proofreading Notes

✓ Rule	Example	Notes
☐		
☐		
☐		
☐		
☐		
☐		
☐		

Proofreading Notes

✓	Rule	Example	Notes
☐			
☐			
☐			
☐			
☐			
☐			
☐			